# Lessons from Ezra

Ted Murray

**Scripture Truth Publications**

# LESSONS FROM EZRA

First published as articles in the magazine "Scripture Truth" 2002-04

FIRST EDITION

FIRST PUBLISHED March 2007

ISBN: 978-0-901860-75-0

© Copyright 2007 Scripture Truth

A publication of Scripture Truth

Scripture quotations, unless otherwise indicated, are taken from The Authorized (King James) Version. Rights in the Authorized Version are vested in the Crown. Reproduced by permission of the Crown's patentee, Cambridge University Press.

Scripture quotations marked (NIV) are taken from the HOLY BIBLE, NEW INTERNATIONAL VERSION. Copyright © 1973, 1978, 1984, International Bible Society. Used by permission of Hodder & Stoughton Publishers, a member of the Hodder Headline Group. All rights reserved. "NIV" is a registered trademark of International Bible Society. UK trademark number 1448790.

Scripture quotations marked "JND Trans." are taken from "The Holy Scriptures, a New Translation from the Original Languages" by J. N. Darby (G Morrish, 1890)

Scripture quotations marked (NKJV) are taken from the New King James Version®. Copyright © 1982 by Thomas Nelson, Inc. Used by permission. All rights reserved.

Cover photograph ©iStockphoto.com/alexsl (Alex Slobodkin)

Published by Scripture Truth Publications
Coopies Way, Coopies Lane,
Morpeth, Northumberland, NE61 6JN

*Scripture Truth is an imprint of Central Bible Hammond Trust, a charitable trust*

Typesetting by John Rice
Printed by Lightning Source

# Contents

# LESSONS FROM EZRA

# Introduction

There are important lessons for today to be learned from the book of Ezra. It can conveniently be divided into two sections: Ezra the Book (chapters 1-6) and Ezra the Man (chapters 7-10). The book is in the historical section of the Bible and is often dismissed as Jewish history with little relevance for today. On further examination we find, however, that it has many lessons from which we at the beginning of the 21st century can benefit.

The book deals with that period at the end of Judah's captivity in Babylon. Together with Nehemiah and Esther, it gives the historical details of the time. Haggai, Zechariah and Malachi are the prophetic books of the period. Daniel stands alone, being both historical and prophetic.

# LESSONS FROM EZRA

## Part 1

# Ezra the Book

### Chapters 1 to 6

# LESSONS FROM EZRA

# Chapter 1:
# The circumstances

### THE FULFILMENT OF GOD'S PROMISE

It is profitable to look into the circumstances prevailing at the time. The Jewish nation had experienced seventy years of captivity. On the throne was a new king, who had been named by Isaiah even before the captivity began. Now God fulfils Jeremiah's prophecy regarding the duration of the captivity. The new king, Cyrus, proclaims a decree that the Jewish remnant be allowed to return to the land of Israel. God's sovereign will was being carried out even by this powerful monarch. What encouragement this must have been to those captives who, like Daniel, were waiting for the fulfilment of God's promise through the prophets. We today can also be encouraged as we read of this historic event, realising that Israel's God is ours and that His purposes are still being carried out!

### OBEDIENCE TO GOD'S WORD

Chapter 1 gives us Cyrus's decree and the preparations made by the remnant to leave Babylon. In verse 2, we read the title 'The LORD God of heaven', which Cyrus used to describe God and to ascribe to Him that rightful sover-

eignty. This is the title which God took when His throne
was removed from the earth and His people given into the
hands of the Gentiles. Although heaven is the domain
where God exercises His full authority, Cyrus acknowledges that God had given him authority over the Persian
empire and had delegated him to build a house for God
at Jerusalem.

Here we have a lesson in obedience to the prompting of
God. Cyrus was stirred in spirit and immediately issued
his remarkable decree. He did not wait for a more convenient time; he did not assemble his advisors. He did
what God laid on his heart! There are times when the
Lord stirs our spirits to do some service for Himself. How
often we fail when we look for the approval of others
before getting on with it.

## VOLUNTEERS FOR GOD

Cyrus's decree is quite remarkable. We do not read of
coercion, but rather a request was made for volunteers.
The volunteers were to separate themselves from the comforts of Babylon to endure hardship in a land which was
desolate. Jerusalem was in ruins, burned out, and from
Nehemiah's account, it consisted of a heap of stones. The
broken-down condition of Jerusalem is a picture of
Christendom today. But there were those who were prepared to endure hardship, to make that unknown journey
back to what had been the place of worship and testimony. One of the lessons we learn from this chapter is
that the path of separation cannot be forced upon a company. It is the response of individuals, not a company, to
the prompting of the Lord to walk the path which He has
revealed.

## SEPARATION UNTO GOD

We see this principle established in Cyrus's decree. As an absolute monarch, he could have rounded up as many Jews as he thought necessary to build the house in Jerusalem. He did not do this. He made a request and issued a challenge: "Who is there among you of all His people? his God be with him, and let him go up to Jerusalem" (verse 3). In this verse we see: (a) the call for separation; (b) the blessing of separation; (c) the place of separation and (d) the reason for separation.

The Christian is called to leave the things of this world: "Love not the world, neither the things that are in the world" (1 John 2:15). This is the negative side of separation. The fact that the Christian is called to go outside the camp where Christ is (Hebrews 13:13) is the positive side of separation. The blessing is the Lord's own promise: "Where two or three are gathered together in my name, there am I in the midst of them" (Matthew 18:20) and "I will never leave you nor forsake you" (Hebrews 13:5, NKJV). The place is where His name is honoured and where He is given the pre-eminence. The reason is for a testimony in this world.

## GOD'S PROVISION FOR WORSHIP

We find that those who took up the challenge were immediately strengthened (verse 6) and, no doubt, encouraged by the resources given to them. Cyrus separated out the vessels which had been taken from the Temple and gave them to Sheshbazzar (his Chaldean name. In chapter 2, he is given his Hebrew name, Zerubbabel, prince of Judah). We should note that it was Mithredath, the Medo-Persian treasurer, who formally and with due solemnity handed over the vessels to Zerubbabel, who was of David's line. The act is an initial fulfilment of Jeremiah 27:22 and foreshadows that future day when the Lord Jesus Christ receives tribute from the nations. The vessels numbered 5,400 pieces; the details of 2,499 pieces are given. This teaches us the importance which God gives to detail. Even the knives are noted in God's record! In this day of casualness, it is a reminder that we should be careful in our stewardship for the Lord. In a future day, we shall have to give account to Him of all that we do.

These utensils, which had formerly been used by the priests in Jerusalem in the daily worship, were restored so that the revival of that divinely appointed form of worship could once more take place. God does not leave His people destitute; He provides what is needed so that He may be worshipped. Can we see in this act some parallel in what takes place when we meet in simplicity for the remembrance of the Lord?

Zerubbabel means 'a stranger in Babel'. No lordliness was found in him; he was a meek man. He did not appear to have any pomp in his make-up. There was no outward show of gift, but he was a faithful man who had the confidence of the ruler and the people. We need today to show these same characteristics and we should seek the Lord's help that this be so. It is wonderful to see that, in the day of breakdown, God has a man who is able to lead.

*"We follow Thee, our Guide, who didst salvation bring:*
*We follow Thee, through grace supplied from heaven's*
*eternal spring."*

# Chapter 2:
# The people

## GOD TAKES NOTE

If in chapter 1 we had the circumstances, in chapter 2 we have the people and another list from God's record. It appears that this is an important record. It is duplicated in Nehemiah 7 and is used as a basis in Nehemiah 3 which records the details of the work which each accomplished. It is not a long list but it does contain the names of all those who went back to Jerusalem, God's centre at that time. The people numbered 42,360 besides servants and 200 choristers, giving a total of 49,897 persons. They appear to have gone back in family units. We see here the importance which God places on the family, and the influence of its head (see 1 Timothy 3:4,5).

Yet even this crowd is few compared to those who originally came out of Egypt – perhaps 1-2 million. This little company turned their backs on the comforts of Babylon where they had been unable to sing the Lord's songs in that strange land (see Psalm 137). This may speak of the relative few in Christendom who are prepared faithfully to follow the path of separation unto the Lord.

The men of Anathoth are an encouraging reminder of the fact that God's word stands sure. Anathoth was the place purchased by Jeremiah as a sign that the land would be restored (Jeremiah 32). These men of Anathoth were able to benefit from the title deeds and see the fulfilment of God's faithfulness.

## RESPONSIBILITY FOR THE SERVICE OF GOD

From verses 36-39, we learn that there were 4,289 priests. Approximately one tenth, then, of the remnant who returned were able to serve in the Temple. These men, along with the Levites, had no inheritance to go back to but they were able to serve the Lord in the way and in the place He had appointed.

Only a few Levites returned. In the time of Solomon, the Levites numbered 38,000 and had an important part to play in the functioning of the Temple worship. Theirs was the responsibility of administering the stores, the tithes, the work of the house of God, the safety of the Temple, the teaching of the Law, and the leading of the praise. But now there are only 74 of them!

Today, there is a similar dearth of those willing to take up responsibility for the upkeep of the testimony of the Lord and maintenance of the fabric. The story is the same throughout Christendom. Surely we should be asking ourselves whether we are amongst the doers or amongst those who stand to one side and criticise. There is still a great need for those who can take their full part in the life of the local church. In Zerubbabel's day, the Levites had nothing to which to look forward, when they returned to the land, other than their individual desire to serve and to please the Lord in His divinely appointed way. They went back in faith, counting on the blessing of the Lord.

## Sing unto the Lord

Next come the singers, the sons of Asaph. They were the leaders of praise; 128 are recorded. Here we find that singing is not the exclusive right of men in the praise of God. Towards the end of the chapter, the choir grows to 200 by the inclusion of the singing women. Both are needed to make up the harmony and thus enhance the note of praise. It is good to realise that some can use the natural gift of a pleasant voice, under the direction of the Holy Spirit, to praise the Lord and make a harmonious sound which brings pleasure to God and the church.

## Labour for God

The Nethinim and Solomon's servants were a group of people who had nothing whatsoever to which to go back. In Solomon's day they were servants. The former may have been descendants of the wily Gibeonites imported by Solomon for the work of building the Temple and his houses, hewers of wood and drawers of water. But here is a group of people, however skilled or lowly in origin, who were prepared to leave their place of leisure for the place of labour for God.

## True to God

Verses 59-61 records those who could not show their genealogy. These people of uncertain origin formed a significant part of the company – 652 persons who could not give a satisfactory account of their history. There are those today who show a zeal for the Lord but are unable to give a clear scriptural answer as to what drives them or how they became Christians. It is good to know that "The Lord knoweth them that are his" (2 Timothy 2:19).

The chapter continues in the same vein, listing the priests who could not fully establish their title to serve in the

Temple. These men and their families took the name of Barzillai, the friend of David. Barzillai had sustained David when he was in trouble but refused to avail himself of David's provisions (2 Samuel 19:32-34). He was blessed by David (verse 39), who later instructed Solomon to provide for Barzillai's sons (1 Kings 2:7). Here we find people showing allegiance to God but wanting to fulfil a service for which they had neither the credentials nor the qualifications. The outcome was that they were barred by the Tirshatha (the governor) from eating of the holy things until there was a priest who could decide the matter with the Urim and Thummin. This could correspond today with those who want to take a place of leadership but cannot fulfil the scriptural requirements (see 1 Timothy 3). There are also those who claim to be saved and apparently know the Lord but have a lifestyle which is contrary to biblical teaching. Though we do not have apostles to give their judgment, as in the early Church, we do have the scriptures to guide us and we should abide by them.

## GIVING TO GOD

At the end of the chapter, we are given the number of those who left Babylon. It is interesting to note the smaller number of servants. This implies that there were a great number of people of substance in the material sense who were no longer prepared to invest their substance and time in the affairs of Babylon but who wanted to throw in their lot with the small remnant and share in the restoration of the testimony in Jerusalem.

Another point of interest is that only beasts of burden are listed: horses, mules, camels and asses. All these animals would help the progress of the return journey. Cattle, sheep and goats tend by their nature to impede progress and would have to be left behind. From this we learn that some hard decisions may have to be made when we take up service for the Lord.

At the end of the chapter, there are gems of encouragement for us today. What did the remnant see when they came to the house of the Lord (verse 68)? Only ruins! But they had a God-given vision and, from their abundance, gave more. This was not a tenth, the tithe according to the Law, but 'after their ability'. Surely the Lord loves a cheerful giver (2 Corinthians 9:7). Here the Lord takes note of those who were moved when they saw what had to be done and who provided some of the means to do it.

### ALL THE PEOPLE OF GOD

The chapter closes with God seeing this weak remnant, a company occupying the ground of all Israel. It is not possible today to gather the whole Church of God in one visible unity. It is possible, however, for even a feeble few to meet on the ground of the Church of God, without sectarian tags and traditions, endeavouring to keep the unity of the Spirit in the bond of peace (Ephesians 4:3).

It should be noted that this unity of the Spirit is broken by discord and cannot be legally enforced. It is our responsibility to act on this with those who seek peace with all men and holiness, without which no man shall see the Lord (Hebrews 12:14). The truth of the One Body (1 Corinthians 10:16) indicates that there is only one, comprising all true believers. Are we to recognise another body, or a narrower circle, than that which we are brought into by the Lord? In principle, we should recognise all believers. Christian fellowship must, if scripturally sound, embrace all believers. In the profession of Christendom there are sadly those, as in Ezra's day, whose records do not stand up. Our fellowship is with those who follow right-

17

eousness, faith, love, peace and who call on the name of the Lord out of a pure heart (2 Timothy 2:19-22).

# Chapter 3:
# The place of worship

In this chapter, obedience is a key feature of the returning remnant of Israel. The people wanted to be in God's centre, Jerusalem. They were marked by devotion to God. They had no homes to move into. There was no beautiful building in which to worship God. Everything was in ruins.

We have no indication of the time which elapsed between the end of chapter 2 and the beginning of chapter 3. We must assume that they had built some form of shelter for their families. They then made preparation for the rebuilding of the temple by clearing away the rubbish which had been strewn around the temple area. This would remind us of the importance of both the home and the place of worship. The home is the place of influence on the family and should be the place where children first hear about the Lord. We are reminded of the influence which Timothy's mother and grandmother had on him (2 Timothy 1:5).

## GIVING GOD HIS PLACE

The site of the temple having been cleared, but the foundations not yet laid, the people built the altar of God (verse 2). We do not find any of man's innovations here, but that the people searched the Scriptures and were guided by "as it is written in the law of Moses". The leaders and the people accepted the authority of Scripture and were obedient to it. Here is yet another lesson for today. So many, today, are apt to look for modern man's thoughts on a given matter or, in some cases, to put more weight on tradition rather than on what Scripture teaches. The people gave priority to the worship of God and God honoured this desire.

The chapter starts with the words "And when the seventh month was come". This was the month when the Jews were to celebrate three feasts of Jehovah – the feast of Trumpets, the Day of atonement, and the feast of Tabernacles (Leviticus 23). These feasts remind us of repentance, redemption and rejoicing. We are not told in this chapter of the celebration of the first two, but we do read "they kept also the feast of tabernacles" (verse 4).

## GATHERING IN UNITY

It is good to see that the people "gathered themselves together as one man in Jerusalem" (verse 1). Psalm 133 reminds us of the blessing of unity. It is not possible, today, to re-gather the whole Church of God in one visible unity. But it is still possible for even a few believers to meet on the ground of the Church of God, without sectarian tags and traditions, endeavouring to keep the unity of the Spirit in the bond of peace (Ephesians 4:3).

We should remember that the unity of the Spirit cannot simply be legally enforced and is broken by discord. During the last few years, so many of God's people have experienced a lot of discord amongst themselves. This has been mainly due to some wanting to rule and thereby enforce a man-made unity. The sad consequences of such actions are all too evident. Thankfully, we do have a remedy. We find that unity is maintained by those who seek "peace with all men, and holiness, without which no man shall see the Lord" (Hebrews 12:14).

In verse 5, we read that they offered the continual burnt offering. That offering prefigured Christ offering Himself without sin to God and, as such, brought pleasure to God (Leviticus 1). It was offered up morning and evening daily. There were no dissenting thoughts or voices to this offering. The people were at one in worship. They appreciated the fact that, in this scene of breakdown and discouragement, there was a continual offering being made to God.

We also read that everyone was willing to make freewill offerings unto the LORD (verse 5). There was nothing lacking. The lesson for us today surely is that if the effort is made and we willingly give more of our time, leisure and wealth to the Lord, He will add His blessing and prosper the testimony of His people. The people of Zerubbabel's day took heed to God's word. They did not deviate from the instructions given by God to Moses but followed them to the letter.

The problem today is that so often we want to have our ideas incorporated into the way we worship. The simplicity of New Testament teaching has been embroidered with our ideas of order, procedure, on how and when we should remember the Lord. Thankfully, amidst the breakdown of the day in which we find ourselves, it is still possible to meet in simplicity, having fellowship with all who call upon the Lord with a pure heart.

Other feasts were also celebrated. The New Moons and all the set feasts were re-established according to all that had been written. There was no holding back. There was an eagerness and an enthusiasm to re-establish what had been lost. Would to God that we in our day had something of their spirit! We seem to be beset with life's problems, with family commitments and with other things which tend to detract and deflect us from giving our all to the Lord. Paul reminded the Colossians that Christ must have the pre-eminence (1:18). On our part, we are happy to quote this verse but are more often than not reluctant to obey it.

### REBUILDING THE TEMPLE

This section, verses 4-7, ends on the happy note that provisions were also made for the various items required for the establishment of the temple. This would remind us of our obligation to meet the needs for the furtherance of the Gospel.

The place of witness and worship was in ruins but they came to the "house of God" (verse 8). The enemies of God had joined together in an attempt to bring to naught that which was for God in this world. We can rejoice that, even in a situation like this, God's purposes are never thwarted. His witness to the world is ever sure, even in a day of breakdown.

We should remind ourselves that "the house of God, which is the church of the living God," is also "the pillar and ground of the truth" (1 Timothy 3:15). Today, we can encourage ourselves in the fact that although much of the truth as to the Church was lost during what we call the dark ages, it has been recovered thanks to faithful men. These men and women turned from human traditions to the living Christ, despite persecution and martyrdom. This treasure has been handed down to us in our day though, sad to say, there are many who have little or no appreciation of its value. The breaking of bread is looked upon as just another way of celebrating the Eucharist. That remembrance feast, when one's heart and mind are engaged with the beauties and glories of our living Lord, leading us on to worship of the Father, is surely a taste of heaven on earth.

We noticed that other set feasts were revived. These feasts surely speak to us of fellowship – those times of joy, sharing with one another the blessings which God has bestowed upon His own. We live in a day when meetings for fellowship and the ministry of God's word are neglected by many. The pressures of modern life are making terrible inroads into the life and wellbeing of the assemblies of God's people. By contrast, it is noticeable that the temples of merchandise are well attended, by saint and sinner alike, in this day of affluence!

## TOGETHER IN WORSHIP

The key word of this chapter is 'together', a word which surely speaks of fellowship. It is used three times: "gathered themselves together" (verse 1); they "stood... together, to set forward the workmen" (verse 9); "they sang together" (verse 11). What a message for us today! If, because of spiritual pride, we cannot gather together, there is no way that the work in the assemblies can progress. As a result of that inactivity, there will be no real singing.

This remnant realised the necessity of fellowship with one another in the Lord's work and the result was manifested for all to see and hear. The recovery was a source of great joy and praise. At the end of this chapter, we read of shouts of joy and cries of sorrow being heard afar off (verses 11-13). The two could not be distinguished. In praise and testimony, there is room for the vitality of the young and also the memories of the old. Both voices should be audible. They are not discordant but blend into one magnificent note which those around have to take account of.

What noise are we making amongst the break-up of today? Is it joy mingled with a sense of sorrow or is it that of discord and argument? The people of God in this chapter were bound together in one common task. They desired to praise and worship God and to let it be known to all around that God was given His rightful place in their midst.

# Chapter 4:
# Difficult days

Believers today can readily identify with the situations encountered by the people of God in this chapter. Here we have two attacks on the Jewish remnant, both motivated by Satan. In the first attack, with the offer of help in the rebuilding of the temple (verse 2), we see how insidious are Satan's wiles. In the second, we have a direct attack on the remnant as a result of their having rejected the offer of help from those whom Scripture describes as "adversaries" (verse 1).

## Satan's deceit

These adversaries were the descendants of a people brought into the land by the Assyrians after they had carried away the ten tribes. At the command of the Assyrian king, these people in Samaria were taught to worship God by one of Jeroboam's priests. Sadly, they then compromised the teaching of these captive priests by fearing the LORD yet serving their own gods (2 Kings 17). The Samaritans of that day can be likened to some in Christendom today who have a form of Christian worship but deny the fundamental truths of the Gospel. They do not accept the word of God in its entirety; they deny the virgin birth and the deity of Christ; they walk in a wordly fashion.

The example in our chapter shows how we should deal with this type of help. Zerubbabel, Joshua, and the leaders of the remnant refused the alliance which had been proposed, thus maintaining the principle of separation. In this way, they declared that they were wholly for God, in spite of the attractiveness of the help of these Samaritans who, as stated in verse 1, were in reality adversaries. Today, we should be aware of this insidious way in which Satan attacks the church.

At the end of chapter 3, the people were full of joy. The Lord had blessed their efforts to lay the foundations of the temple. Satan chooses just such a moment to launch his attack. We need to be careful of so-called offers of help and not be afraid to refuse such. Zerubbabel's answer was very clear: "You may do nothing with us to build a house for our God; but we alone will build to the LORD God of Israel, as King Cyrus the king of Persia has commanded us" (verse 3). Through this action of the leaders, the remnant was maintained in a path of separation, the neglect of which in the past had been the cause of all their trouble. Had they agreed to this offer, the work would have been ruined from the start. The end of the book of Nehemiah plainly shows the failure which spoiled the results of that which started so well.

We only have to look into church history to see similar examples of failure through compromise. The Reformation started out well but fell very short of what might have been had some of the leaders not made alliances with secular persons and powers. The results of these alliances are a sad record of wars and intrigues which beset the church. Revelation 17 shows us the terrible result of religion compromising with secular powers and politics. Believers today need to realise that we cannot compromise with a Christless profession or a godless society. In today's climate of pluralism, we need to take care to be independent of the world's systems and thus be separated unto the Lord (2 Corinthians 6:17,18).

## SATAN'S ONSLAUGHT

For the remnant, the watchword was separation, not compromise. This resulted, as we see later in this chapter, in a more intense form of opposition. The situation is the same today as it was in Zerubbabel's day. If true believers maintain a path of separation from the world, opposition will follow. If the path taken is compromise, then opposition may be avoided, but the power to live a life for Christ will be greatly diminished. We should realise that a life lived for the service of the Lord will result in some persecution: "All that will live godly in Christ Jesus shall suffer persecution" (2 Timothy 3:12). Persecution does not always take on a physical character but has many forms and affects the believer in numerous ways. Satan has had a lot of experience in this field and knows all our weaknesses.

The opposition grew (verses 4,5) and was persistent. In verses 5-7, we learn that the opposition lasted from the days of Cyrus to those of Darius. In between these kings came Ahasuerus (not the one mentioned in the book of Esther), but known as Cambeses in secular history. It seems as though the opposition had little success during the time of these kings. The remnant stood firm, carrying on the task which they had started with a firm conviction that they were carrying out the will of God and the command of the king.

Artaxerxes now comes into the picture. He is identified as the usurper and also known as Smerdis. Having seized the throne, he would be very much disposed to annul the decrees of his predecessors, so establishing his authority. The opposition see their chance and write a letter. From 4:6 to 6:18, the language used is Chaldean or Aramaic. These are the actual transcripts of the letters which passed to and fro.

The letter to Artaxerxes is a misrepresentation of the truth as to what was happening. Today, it would be called spin. It was what they thought the king would like to hear and, from what we read from verse 17 onwards, it had its desired effect. In the letter, they profess a great concern for the king's interests and express their fear that his taxes would not be paid and he would lose his dominion beyond the river. They then stretch the truth, stating that the Jews are rebuilding the walls and the city. Some of the houses in Jerusalem may have been rebuilt (Haggai 1:4), but permission for the rebuilding of the walls was not given until the days of Nehemiah.

This remnant, under Zerubbabel and Joshua, were not bent on building reputations for themselves, but were establishing a place of testimony and worship in the place the LORD God of Israel had commanded through Cyrus. We are reminded of the Lord's words: "Seek ye first the kingdom of God" (Matthew 6:33). So Paul reminds us that Christ must have the pre-eminence in all things (Colossians 1:18).

We then read of the cunning way in which their enemies displayed the dirty washing of Israel's past. We cannot hide our dirty washing. It behoves us, as Christians, to walk circumspectly in this present evil world (Galatians 1:4). Christians today are often besmirched by the acts of those who profess Christianity but do not practise it. The unfaithfulness of Zedekiah and others of the kings prior to the captivity was used to good effect by the accusers. Verse 17 onwards records the king's answer. The work was stopped by force of arms even though the edict of Cyrus had not been revoked. The work ceased until the second year of Darius, king of Persia (verse 24). To the casual observer, it might appear that the work of God was defeated. We should take heart in the fact that God's purposes cannot be put to one side. The One who is the Alpha and the Omega has the last say.

Sadly, what happened from the time the work ceased until it was re-established is something we are all accustomed to. It is called apathy. We see it creeping in in the first of the letters to the seven churches, and finally rampant in the seventh letter (Revelation chapters 2,3). It appears that, in this intervening period, the Jews looked to their own comforts. They built their panelled houses, stored up their goods, and carefully looked after their own interests. There is no suggestion that their adversaries caused any suffering to the Jews during the time they were looking after their own comforts.

So it is today. We can work all the hours that are available. We are encouraged to make our own way in our chosen careers. If we are sports minded, this is also encouraged. The world will have nothing to say against all these things. But in making these our aims in life, we are not fully engaged in the work of the Lord. The thing that offends the world is to see the claims of Christ being met – to see Christians energised by the Spirit, their light no longer hidden under a bushel, but shining brightly. This exposes the selfishness, pride, hypocrisy, and the other evils that are present in the world.

Thankfully, the work was re-started, as chapters 5,6 record. Let us be encouraged that our God "is able to do exceeding abundantly above all that we ask or think, according to the power that worketh in us. Unto him be glory in the church by Christ Jesus throughout all ages, world without end. Amen" (Ephesians 3:20,21).

# Chapter 5:
# The reawakening

## TIME TO START AGAIN

Some fifteen years have passed since the events of chapter 4. Nothing appears to be happening but, behind the scenes, God is working! God has two prophets, Haggai and Zechariah, in the background and, at the right time, they are used of God to stir up the people. The people were in the right position, but not in the right condition. They were in the right place, Jerusalem, that the Lord would have them, but their condition was such that they had stopped the rebuilding work on the temple.

As time passes, we, too, are apt to let some things slip. Our fervour wanes, our desire for the Lord's testimony diminishes and, as a consequence, we become dismayed and discouraged. God's word had started the work (Ezra 1:1), and only God's word would continue it (Galatians 3:3). When the Lord wants something doing, He gives instructions through His word. Because of our unbelief, we do not see the power of His word. We allow our human reasoning to influence our belief and, consequently, we miss out on the blessing.

God always has the remedy. His two prophets bring His word to the people. Their message was in the form of the stick and the carrot. Haggai first rebukes, then instructs and, finally, encourages. Zechariah first of all encourages but then speaks of future events. These two prophets were used of God to tell forth, and to foretell, His message to the remnant in Jerusalem. The result of this was that the decree of the pagan king, Artaxerxes, was set aside and the people bowed to the power of God's declared word. The people heard the word, obeyed the word, and so found their fear and dismay banished. They were prepared to do not only the physical work required but they also were not ashamed to declare to those opposing them the names of those who were involved in the rebuilding. Are we, in our day, prepared to be identified as, and associated with, those who follow God's Christ?

## THE MESSAGES OF HAGGAI AND ZECHARIAH

The prophetic messages given were accepted by the elders who, in turn, instructed the people to restart the work of rebuilding the house of God (verse 2). Haggai gives four messages over a period of four months (see Haggai 1:1; 2:1,10,20). The first message, a rebuke, took almost a month to have an effect. No one likes to be rebuked, but here we see the working of God in the conscience of the people. We, too, have to admit that it often takes time for the word of God to have its effect on us. Like the remnant, we tend to pay more attention to our domestic affairs than to the testimony of God. Haggai's second message is one of encouragement: "Be strong" (2:4). His next message is one of instruction on how to live a clean life, a life separate from defilement (see 1 John 2:15). His final message was one of promise, looking forward to the day when the Davidic covenant would be fulfilled. That day, when the Lord will reign as King of kings, is yet to come.

While Haggai's ministry focussed largely on practical issues, Zechariah's ministry focussed on Jerusalem which is mentioned over 40 times in the book. Its key statement is, "I am zealous for Jerusalem and for Zion with a great jealousy" (1:14). The book's 14 chapters cover 8 visions (chapters 1-6), fasting and traditions, ( chapters 7-8), and two 'burdens' or deeply felt messages from God ( chapters 9-14). The preaching of God's word had its effect – the people were encouraged, invigorated, and restarted the work.

We see something of God's grace and His care in verse 5 of our chapter: "The eye of their God was upon…them". Surely we should take heart in our day that that same eye of our God, which is even upon the sparrow (Luke 12:6), is upon us also. If we would realise that God is for us (Romans 8:31), then nothing would deter us from being fully committed to the testimony of the Lord.

## THE ENEMY AT WORK

Another adversary is now brought into the picture (verse 3). Although time passes, and people come and go from the scene, the attack never ceases. The implication from verse 8 is that Tattenai and his companion, Shethar-Bozenai, came across the re-building by chance. We must realise that, by contrast, the one who is our enemy, the prince and power of the air, is fully aware of our every action and will do his utmost, either personally or through his agents, to hinder any work for God in which we are engaged.

It is interesting to note that the enemy does not use false evidence concerning the re-building of the city: "the work goes on and prospers in their hands". Even the accuser of the brethren cannot deny the facts! When the work of the Lord proceeds and souls are won for Him, worship pours forth from grateful hearts. Even Satan cannot deny that which is for the Lord's glory and honour. The remnant's fearless testimony is recorded: "We are the servants of the God of heaven and earth" (verse 11). Although Israel's failure, and God's judgment upon them, are recorded, this no longer affected their work for the Lord. On the contrary, the effect of God's word through His messengers enabled the remnant to carry on. Let us take heed to the word of the Lord in our day and strengthen the things that remain.

## THE PEOPLE'S CONFIDENCE

It is noticeable that, when challenged, the people gave their answer in a two-fold way: they spoke of being servants of God and also of being servants, in a political sense, of the king (verse 13). There may be a lesson for us in our day that we should be aware of what is available to us, as Christians, from governments of the day and should utilise these benefits to the full. F. B. Hole writes, "This Darius, of the ancient line, was inclined to reverse the edicts of the usurper, Artaxerxes. On checking the records, he found the truth of the matter and, as requested, sent his pleasure."

The psalmist reminds us that God's truth will be our shield and buckler (Psalm 91:4). John 8:32 reminds us that the truth will make us free. Here we see the application of these wonderful scriptures and, in the next chapter, we see the outcome of the search, instigated by the opposition and commissioned by Darius, resulting in the benefit of God's people. God will never fail faith in Him. He does, and will continue, to make bare His arm on behalf of those who acknowledge the authority of His word (Isaiah 52:10). Here God causes the wrath of men to praise Him and to fulfil His word (Psalm 76:10).

# Chapter 6:
# The building finished

## GOD'S ANSWER

When the original decree was found and checked, it was found to be more favourable to the Jews than to their adversaries! Verses 1-5 detail the search for, and the location of, Cyrus's scroll and also the king's command, "Let the House be re-built!" We also find the purpose of the building, how the building should be done, together with the materials which had to be provided. What a relief it must have been to the remnant of that day when Darius's reply was received! What a triumph of God's grace towards His faithful people who had not ceased working but had stated that they would await the answer of the king. Their faith had been tested throughout the considerable time which would have elapsed before the reply was received.

There are times in our lives when we have to wait for God's answer. When it comes, we may be full of praise and worship to the One who is the Spring and Source of our blessing, even when that answer is not always the one we expect! What a shock for Tattenai and his companions! Not only were they forbidden to hinder the work, but they had to provide for it! The lines from the hymn, "God moves in a mysterious way, His wonders to perform", certainly sum up the situation here. We might take courage as we ponder these scriptures and note that, when everything seems hopeless, God's mighty hand is revealed. What an outcome we have here! Not only were the adversaries to assist in the provision of the materials needed, they would also suffer the consequences if they disobeyed the king's command.

In verses 7-22, we see how God deals with His people through circumstances. In verse 7, there is the command to "let...alone", God's protecting hand. In verse 8, "Let the cost be paid immediately", God's providing hand. In verse 9, "Whatever is needed for worship, give daily without fail", God's bountiful hand. In verse 10, "that they may offer", God's sustaining hand. Finally, in verses 11,12, "I have made a decree, that whosoever shall alter this word...", God's hand of judgment. We see the hand of God's judgment, in fulfilment of Darius's curse, in what happened to Antiochus who defiled the temple and died. The Romans, too, who utterly destroyed the temple, have gone, their empire but a memory. God is not mocked. His word will not return to Him void "but shall accomplish that which I please, and it shall prosper in the thing whereto I sent it" (Isaiah 55:11).

## GOD'S MESSAGE

What a relief for the people of that day when they not only heard the outcome of the letters, but saw the results! Tattenai and his associates promptly obeyed the command of Darius. As the elders of the Jews built, they prospered from the ministry of Haggai and Zechariah (verse 14). This is the second time that these two men have been mentioned. Lessons have already been drawn from their ministry, as we saw in the previous chapter. There is further instruction here.

In verse 14, the title 'prophet' is only given to Haggai. To our way of thinking, Zechariah would more readily merit the title, as it is he who unfolds future events. We have to realise that a prophet is one who declares God's message from heaven to men on earth, whatever the character of that message. "He that prophesieth speaketh unto men to edification, and exhortation, and comfort" (1 Corinthians 14:3). This is exactly what Haggai did. He reminded, cajoled, encouraged, and motivated the people by his ministry. He was God's messenger for the moment. Zechariah's message was equally important giving hope for the future of Israel.

Today, we are more likely to enjoy a message similar to that of Zechariah than that of Haggai. No one likes being told what to do; we are far happier considering future events and other doctrinal matters than doing the work of the present. Today, we need to heed the call to restart the work of evangelisation. The hymn writer reminds us that, although the foundation is laid on the Living Stone, the fabric of the building is a continuous process.

> *View the vast building, see it rise;*
> *The work how great, the plan how wise!*
> *Oh, wondrous fabric, power unknown,*
> *That rears it on the "Living Stone"!*

It is our task today to realise that there is work to do on building the church. We are the labourers and skilled workers whom God wants to use and will use if we are prepared to work for Him.

## Finished at last!

So the work was finished (verse 15). It had taken a long time, some twenty years or more to complete. Surely this is a message of encouragement that, despite the barren years, the work was finished. Let us take hold of the fact that God's great work, which is according to His wise plan, will be carried out. It is our privilege to be part of His workforce today. We can share in the joy of being used of God to carry out His plan. So the people celebrated the dedication of the temple with joy (verse 16). They rejoiced and offered sacrifices at the dedication, but they also remembered their failings. As well as the animals offered as a peace offering, we find that they offered 12 goats as a sin offering for all Israel. The remnant in Jerusalem were mindful of the whole nation. In the days of breakdown in which we live, we should be mindful of the whole Church of God, not just the few with whom we fellowship on a regular basis.

At the end of verse 18, we are reminded that they were obedient to the written word. The phrase "as it is written" is a timely reminder to us today. If we accepted God's word at its face value, instead of looking for other opinions, there would be less controversy amongst the people of God. It would also safeguard us from the wiles of Satan. When the Lord was tempted in the wilderness, He used the written word to repel Satan's assault.

## Holy unto the Lord

We need to be able not just to quote chapter and verse, but to be governed by, and to live according to, the living word of God. When the remnant celebrated the Passover on the fourteenth day of the first month, we see a people governed by, and living according to, God's word (verse 19). In verses 20,21, the priests, the Levites, the remnant, and others who had separated themselves from the filth of the nations joined in this time of revival and blessing. The priests and the Levites purified themselves in order that they could slaughter the Passover lamb for the separated company.

The Passover to the Jew corresponds to the Lord's Supper to the Christian. Both speak of the death of Christ. The Passover reminded the Jews of their deliverance by God from the yoke of Egypt. The Lord's death reminds the Church of the price paid for its redemption. Today, in this dispensation of grace, this principle of personal purification applies to all believers when they come to remember the Lord in His death. Paul reminds us that each one must examine himself and so partake of the Supper (1 Corinthians 11:23-29).

In the company portrayed in our chapter, there is a corporate cleanliness; they were all pure. Today, whilst each believer is positionally cleansed from sin through faith in the finished work of Christ, the day to day defilement in each of our lives must be dealt with. Those who gather together to remember the Lord in His death must be both holy and pure. At the beginning of the church's history, all who called upon the name of the Lord had a place at His table. As time passed, it became necessary to issue instructions that a person living a wicked life was not to partake of the Lord's Supper (1 Corinthians 5). Teachers of false doctrine were also to be identified by the church and denied fellowship (2 John 10). These principles still apply. All who eat unworthily are guilty of the body and blood of the Lord (1 Corinthians 11:27). But we should always remember that it is the Lord's Table, not ours.

In verse 22, we read that all those who had separated themselves from the filthiness of the nations of the land in order to seek the Lord, kept the feast with joy. They had reason to be joyful. They had separated themselves unto the Lord; they had found favour with the king; they could work without fear; their hands had been strengthened. We, too, can enjoy a similar experience to those of Zerubbabel's day when we are in the good of what God has done for us (1 Peter 2:9). Let us rejoice, even in our day, that the Lord ever watches and cares for His own!

*LESSONS FROM EZRA*

## Part 2

# Ezra the Man

## Chapters 7 to 10

*LESSONS FROM EZRA*

# Chapter 7:
# Ezra the man

## His background

Some 78 years have passed since the return of the Jews under Zerubbabel in the reign of Cyrus to Jerusalem, and some 56-58 years since the completion of the Temple. Many of the returned remnant had lost their zeal for God. Some had married and been given in marriage to the people of the land, thereby absorbing their customs. The following generations had very little appreciation of what God had done in bringing them back from Babylon and establishing the centre of worship in Jerusalem.

Nevertheless, God was continuing His work through devout Mordecai and his niece, Esther. Through their faithfulness and courage, God preserved the Jews throughout the Persian empire. Amongst these would be Ezra and Nehemiah. This was also a period of great political significance. The expansion of the Persian empire had been halted by the Greeks at the battles of Marathon, Thermopylae and Salamis.

There is surely a message for us today in this. The Lord's message to the church at Ephesus, "Nevertheless I have

this against you, that you have left your first love"
(Revelation 2:4, NKJV) would remind us how far the
church has fallen and how much ground we have let slip.
Yet it was in just this kind of situation with the Jews that
God raised up His servant, Ezra. We should be encouraged that, in a day of breakdown, God has His servants
who are true to His word and can be used for the restoration of God's testimony.

In chapter 7, Ezra is just such a servant of the Lord. The
chapter opens with another king on the throne. During
his reign, there is another awakening, or perhaps it should
be called a reawakening, of the Jews with God's marked
out servant, Ezra, the leader. The chapter is a wonderful
character study of Ezra. Here we see that, although he had
the confidence of the king, he was identified with the people of God. He was willing to be amongst those who were
willing to sacrifice the comforts of a relatively easy life for
one of hardship in the place where God had set His name.

## His pedigree

Ezra's pedigree is given in verses 1-5. He was probably the
great-great grandson of Seraiah, the High Priest, who was
killed by Nebuchadnezzar (2 Kings 25:18-21). His
genealogy also included Hilkiah who "found the book of
the Law in the house of the LORD" (2 Kings 22:8) and was
responsible for the revival in the days of Josiah. His line,
which included the loyal Zadok who became High Priest
during David's reign, could be traced right back to
Phinehas, whose javelin had turned aside the wrath of
God, and to whom God gave "My covenant of peace" and
to his descendants a covenant of an everlasting priesthood
(Numbers 25:6-13).

Phinehas was a man who was zealous for God. His act had
made atonement for the children of Israel; God rewarded

his faithfulness. We see those same characteristics in Ezra. In our day, we can be thankful for those faithful families who continue to serve the Lord in meekness and godly fear. Timothy had a mother and grandmother who had genuine faith (2 Timothy 1:5). Many today can be thankful for parents, grandparents and, in some cases, great grandparents who, in their generation, made known the message of the Gospel and lived accordingly. Do we, in turn, pass on such a heritage to the generations following?

## HIS ABILITY

Verses 6-10 bear testimony to Ezra. He was a skilled scribe in the Law of Moses. Here was a man who had a deep knowledge of God's word. If we want to be marked out by God for a particular service, we also need to have a good understanding of Scripture. "Your word is a lamp to my feet and a light to my path" (Psalm 119:105, NKJV). Here there is both illumination on the way so that we need not stumble and light surrounding our walk so that others may see and be attracted. People were attracted to Ezra and were prepared to follow him.

Ezra sought the king's permission for himself and his companions to leave Babylon for Jerusalem. "The king granted him all his request, according to the hand of the LORD his God upon him" (verse 6). Here was a man who, being in the secret of God's mind, walked according to God's will. This resulted in God's favour resting upon him and upon those who were prepared with him to suffer the hardship of the testimony to God's name rather than enjoying the ease of Babylon.

It was a long journey, taking four months (verse 9), before they arrived in Jerusalem. Again we read that the good hand of the Lord was upon them. The words suggest that Ezra recognised that, without the Lord's help, he could do

47

nothing. Are we aware that, without that same help, our efforts will also be useless? Unless we have the hand of the Lord upon us, unless we walk by His word and are in His will, our efforts will be unfruitful and become tiresome to us. We will become religious! The lukewarmness which characterised the church at Laodicea will be ours and so will be the consequences (Revelation 3:16).

## HIS ATTITUDE

Ezra prepared his heart to seek the Law of the Lord and to do it (verse 10). This was what developed his abilities. He realised that the Scriptures, which had been graciously preserved during the exile, were given by God. This gave him a reverential appreciation of the sacred text. "The secret of the LORD is with those who fear Him" (Psalm 25:14, NKJV). We should have no less an appreciation. We need constantly to remind ourselves that "All Scripture is given by inspiration of God, and is profitable for doctrine, for reproof, for correction, for instruction in righteousness, that the man of God may be complete, thoroughly equipped for every good work" (2 Timothy 3:16,17, NKJV).

Then, with this reverential fear and godliness, he had studied the Scriptures, diligently and no doubt methodically. He not only read the word but sought out its meaning and purpose. Ezra was marked by a preparedness to apply the Scriptures to his life. His was not just an academic knowledge which might give him a certain kudos. He was a man who scrupulously obeyed the Word of God, lived in the good of it, and was able to fulfil the will of God in his day. "If any man will do His will, he shall know of the doctrine" (John 7:17; see also James 1:25).

The result of continuing and not forgetting, but doing, the word is that blessing follows. Ezra was a good example of a man of the Book. He interpreted, unfolded and taught the meaning of God's word to God's people. The result of the application of that word to his own life was that he was able, and fitted, to teach statutes and ordinances in Israel (verse 10). Do we take time to study the Word of God for ourselves and apply it to our lives, or is our knowledge of it all second-hand? The result of second-hand knowledge can only be weakness.

## HIS REPUTATION

In verses 11 onwards, we see the result of Ezra's petition and the high esteem in which King Artaxerxes held Ezra. The king's letter states that Ezra was the priest and a scribe expert in the commandments of the Lord and His statutes to Israel. In this way, Ezra worshipped, worked and walked in the light of what had been revealed in his studies of the Word of God. The king's letter is remarkable in that it contains not only commendation but also a decree to the people who volunteer to go up to Jerusalem, an instruction, a reminder of the task before them, a passport, provision for the journey and, finally, a direct commission to Ezra from the king. The letter is in Aramaic, the language of the realm.

In His providential ways, God safeguarded Ezra and his companions on the long, hazardous journey to Jerusalem. In chapter 8, Ezra's companions are listed and their faithfulness is noted. Here in chapter 7, the subject is Ezra the man. The letter, however, indicates only a patron and servant relationship between the king and Ezra. It fails to recognise that the hand of the Lord was upon Ezra (verse 28). The letter, although by the hand of the king, was God's doing. The result is a marvellous picture of God's governmental dealings in the restoration of the testimony.

As with Cyrus' decree, there is no coercion of the Jews to leave Babylon. Permission was given to any or all of the people of Israel who volunteered, to go with Ezra. As has already been stated, God does not force His people, but He removes every legal barrier for those who have the heart and the courage to go back to the place where His house has been established. The long sentence in vertses 14-17 is broken up by the word 'whereas'. There is first of all the king's desire to know what is happening in Judea. Then there is the trust that the king and his counsellors had in Ezra to be faithful with the treasures they gave him. Finally, we have the people's confidence in Ezra, entrusting him with their free-will offerings. This all resulted in Ezra and his companions having full liberty to be engaged in the worship and service of the Lord. Moreover, assurance was given that their needs would be met.

God is no man's debtor. Paul's assurance is equally ours today: "My God shall supply all your need according to His riches in glory by Christ Jesus" (Philippians 4:19). That epistle clearly shows how God had provided all that was needed for His service. Although we are responsible to carry out the service of the Lord, we should never forget that God is in charge of the resources. If Romans 12:1 reminds us of our obligations to the Lord, Philippians 4:19 gives us the source of the resources needed to enable us to be fully engaged in that service.

The challenge for us today is whether we are fully aware of what is our "reasonable (or, intelligent) service" and whether we have experienced those resources from the good hand of God. If we were in the good of these things, then we might see greater blessing, resulting in numbers being added to the church. We would be bringing in greater measure "the sacrifice of praise to God, that is, the fruit of our lips, giving thanks to His name" (Hebrews

13:15). Not only would this be a sweet savour unto God, but it would also be an attraction, like the smoke rising from the brazen altar, to those who do not know the Lord.

## HIS JOY

In the final two verses (vertses 27-28), we have an outburst of praise and worship. Ezra gives God all the glory. He can hardly contain himself as he sees God moving the heart of the king to grant him and his companions permission to go to Jerusalem. The realisation that God "is able to do exceedingly abundantly above all that we ask or think, according to the power that works in us" (Ephesians 3:20) was paramount in Ezra's life. Do we have this same confidence? Are we available to the Lord so that He might exhibit His power in us? Paul could write, "I can do all things through Christ who strengthens me" (Philippians 4:13, NKJV).

That power and strength might seem to be somewhat lacking in the church today. It is all too easy to see failure, despondency, breakdown and dwindling numbers. Let us take courage in the fact that the Word of God is still the same, the power of God has not diminished. The Lord, as Head of His Church, is still able to work to His praise and glory, even in this day as He did in Ezra's day.

Ezra realised that it was the mercy of God which had brought about the blessing. That same mercy of God met us when we were dead in our sins (Ephesians 2:4-8). In these verses, we are reminded of the greatness of the riches which have been given us, of the power of God to transform our lives, of the blessing we share with Christ in the heavenly places in order that God might show forth the riches of His grace in a day to come. What a great God we have! Like Ezra, we can say, "The hand of the LORD my God was upon me" (verse 28).

Let us be encouraged as we realise that our Lord Jesus is "the same yesterday, today, and for ever" (Hebrews 13:8). Let us, like Ezra, be willing to allow God to use us. That same Word of God is still our resource, though we possess it in fuller measure than was available to Ezra. It may be that our attitude is not as keen as it once was, that our testimony has become dull. If only we had a reputation like Ezra's! Then, but only then, would we see that same hand of God upon us in blessing. May God challenge our hearts as we read about a man of old who studied, applied, taught, obeyed, and lived in the light of God's Word!

# Chapter 8:
# Ezra's companions

Like chapter 2, chapter 8 consists of a list of names. Less numerous than chapter 2, this list consists only of 1,700 people. The people listed here, like those in chapter 2, share the same desire to be at God's centre, Jerusalem. In chapter 7, we saw how King Artaxerxes was favourably disposed towards the Jews and Ezra in particular. He granted permission to all who volunteered to leave Babylon to return with Ezra to Jerusalem. Chapter 8 opens with the statement, "These are the heads of their fathers' houses". In this article, we shall look at the lessons to be learned from these men and the meanings of their names.

The list of names can be divided into 5 easily recognised groups. Within each group, the names fall into sets of three, with almost all of the heads of families listed bringing with them a number of males. The characteristics of each group, as we shall see, are essential features in every assembly of the Lord's people today. It is important for the proper functioning of the local assembly that these features are be seen. Otherwise, there will be disorder and an unclear testimony. The Lord has given these gifts to believers in every locality. Sadly, they may not always be seen because of discord and dissension and, at times, the dominance of some of those who take the lead in the local assembly. Each of us needs to examine our heart and conduct as to how we display these features.

## GROUP 1 – PRIESTS AND KINGS (VERSE 2)

Here we see something of the responsibility that is ours because of the position we have been brought into by Christ. The first name is Gershom, meaning 'a stranger there', a son of Phineas. The next is Daniel, 'God is Judge', a son of Ithamar, and finally, Hattush, 'a contender', a son of David. Peter reminds us that believers are both a holy and a royal priesthood (1 Peter 2:5,9). As such, we should be characterised by those features indicated in the meanings of these names.

'A stranger there' – are we at home in the world that crucified our Lord? 'God is Judge' – do we realise that we shall all stand before the judgment seat of Christ and give an account of what we have done with the talents entrusted to us in His service? 'Contender' – are we contending in our daily lives for the faith delivered unto us, or have we become lukewarm? As we consider these challenges, surely these features should characterise us in view of what we are in Christ.

## GROUP 2 – MEN OF INFLUENCE (VERSES 3-14)

These verses list the achievements of these men of influence. We need to remember that the Lord takes note of and values what we do for Him. There are five separate groups, each with their own distinguishing features, in these twelve verses. We will consider each of these in turn.

### GOSPEL PREACHERS

In this first group, we find three men: Zechariah, 'Jehovah is renowned'; Elihoenai, 'to Jehovah are mine eyes'; Ben-Jahaziel, 'God reveals'. As we consider the meanings of these three names (in reverse order), we have a picture of how the Holy Spirit works through the preaching of the Gospel. In grace, our situation as sinners is revealed to us; then we are instructed to look to the Lord and be saved; turning our eyes upon Jesus, we finally obtain a lasting impression of His greatness. "The things of the world will grow strangely dim in the light of His glory and grace."

### HELPS

In the second group, we have another three men: Ebed, 'servant'; Jeshaiah, 'Jehovah is my Helper'; and Zebadiah, 'Jehovah endows'. This group typifies those people in the church today who are always able to make time to do the unglamorous and onerous jobs which many of us tend to leave undone. We should remember that the Lord made Himself of no reputation (Philippians 2:7). When we do take on some of these jobs in the assembly, we are often amazed how the Lord gives us the needed strength and endows us with the power to see them through. These men, characterised by humility, are those we should emulate in our day. In their day, there was breakdown but also a glimmer of revival. These men (though numbering only 200) left the comfort of Babylon to endure the hardships of Jerusalem so that they might repair the breakdown and advance that revival. How we need such today! They would surely come into the category of 'helps' (see 1 Corinthians 12:28).

### DEDICATED

The third group brings us another trio: Obadiah, 'servant of Jehovah'; Ben Josiphiah, 'Jehovah adds'; and another

Zechariah, 'Jehovah is renowned'. In this group, we have a picture of dedicated service leading to addition which adds renown, or glory, to the Lord. Dedication is a feature that is sometimes lacking in our service for the Lord. As a result, we no longer see spiritual growth. We read of the early church that "the Lord added to the church daily those who were being saved" (Acts 2:47, NKJV). Where is this growth today? Have we grown accustomed to listening with a critical ear to others minister God's word so that we make sure, like the Pharisees and Scribes, that the ministry is orthodox? Are we concerned only with meeting criteria that have been passed down rather than working out from Scripture by the Spirit's guidance the truth of God for ourselves today?

### APPRECIATIVE

In the fourth group there are four names mentioned: Johanan, 'Jehovah is gracious'; Eliphelet, 'God of escape'; Jeiel, 'God snatches away'; and Shemaiah, 'Jehovah is fame'. The last three are sons of Adonikam, 'my Lord has risen'. The group gives us a picture of appreciation. Each believer has an appreciation of the grace of God (Ephesians 2:8). In Ephesians 1, we are reminded that by grace we are accepted in the Beloved. Our redemption and our forgiveness is according to the riches of His grace. Every blessing that we have is from and of God. What a gracious God we have! We then realise the effect of His great salvation in delivering us from the power of Satan. As a result, we are able to express in worship the fame of our Lord who has risen from the dead.

### FAITHFUL MEN

The fifth group of Ezra's companions consists only of two names: Uthai, 'Jehovah helps' and Zabud, 'well remembered'. It is interesting that Bigvai, their father (verse 14), had already gone up to Jerusalem with Zerubabel (2:2). Here we have a picture of the generations of faithful men. There are those in the church today who, because of their upbringing, have come to know the Lord. Like Timothy, "from childhood [they] have known the Holy Scriptures" (2 Timothy 3:15, NKJV). We can be thankful for faithful examples in families where the different generations follow the Lord. We can also look back with thankfulness to spiritual forebears by whom the Lord has blessed us. Some of these were used to recover truths which had been lost to the church in earlier generations: coming together in simplicity to remember the Lord in the breaking of bread; taking our place as holy and royal priests before God; looking for the coming of the Lord for His Church. What a heritage we come into as we endure the hardship of, but enjoy the blessing of, moving to God's centre! "Outside the camp" is the place where we should be to "offer the sacrifice of praise to God" (Hebrews 13:10-15, NKJV).

## GROUP 3 – MEN OF TRUST (VERSES 15-17)

In verse 15, it seems as if Ezra had a crisis on his hands. The people had camped for three days during which time it was discovered that there was a lack of the sons of Levi for the worship of God. This was a serious problem then as it is today. Too often today we suffer from silent brothers, men who are able to help but somehow manage to remain silent during the long pauses which sometimes occur when we gather in His Name to worship. The men listed in verse 16 are described as "leaders" and "men of understanding". What a blessing it was for Ezra to be able to turn to them for help! Today, we still need men like these who are concerned with the welfare of the assemblies of God's people.

Their names are interesting. Firstly, we have Eliezer, 'God is help'; Ariel, 'lion of God'; Shemaiah, 'Jehovah is fame'. We are reminded of the psalmist's confidence, "My help cometh from the LORD" (Psalm 121:2). In days of difficulty, it is good to remind ourselves that the Lord is our only source of help. When we realise that without Him we can do nothing, then we see something of His might and awesomeness, causing us to rejoice in Him. Acts 27:39-44 is an apt reminder of this.

Then we have Elnathan, 'God is giver'; Nathan, 'giver'; and Zechariah, 'God is renowned'. Their names remind us of where our resources lie, how they are dispensed, and the resulting effect of good stewardship. God's resources are unlimited (see Philippians 4:19; 2 Corinthians 9:8).

The final trio are Meshullam, 'associated friend'; Joiarib, 'Jehovah contends'; and another Elnathan, 'God is giver'. This group would speak to us today of friendship and fellowship in the testimony, but with the reminder that we have to guard the truth and contend against the inroads of false doctrine. When there is that fellowship in truth, then God blesses (see Psalm 133). Both Paul and Jude remind us of the need to be on our guard (1 Timothy 6:20) and to contend for the faith (Jude 3).

These characteristics are very much needed amongst the people of God today. How much we need those, however few, who are able to associate themselves wholeheartedly with the presentation and maintenance of the testimony of the Lord to His praise and honour!

## GROUP 4 – THE LEVITES (VERSES 18-23)

The Levites were those whose privilege it was to minister in the sanctuary. The picture painted in verse 15 was black. "None of the sons of Levi" had been found among them. Ezra, a priest, knowing well the indispensable role of the Levites, discussed the problem with his associates. Those men of trust, whom we considered in the previous section, were used by God to search out Levites, those who were able to carry out the daily duties of the temple. Today the Lord has work to do for every believer. As the hymn puts it, "There's a work for Jesus none but you can do". Each of us needs to examine his or her heart humbly before the Lord as to the time we spend in service for Him.

We seem to live in a day when only occasional attendance to remember the Lord is deemed sufficient. This attitude has almost destroyed the testimony and the joy of fellowship. There is, in some places, a feeling of isolation and despair amongst those who are struggling to maintain that which was once delivered unto them and enjoyed to the full. Let us take heart from this example of Ezra. All was not lost! Three more men, two of them with their families, were found willing to take their place with the Lord's people: Sheribiah, 'Jehovah originates'; Hashabiah, 'Jehovah is associated'; and Jeshiah, 'Jehovah helps'. They were accompanied by the Nethinims, 'dedicated to serve'.

As we ponder these meanings, we can be encouraged that we have the word of God to guide us in how we approach and worship God (John 14:6). We need to let that word of Christ dwell in us richly (Colossians 3:16). On the night of His betrayal, the Lord Jesus promised that we would not be left without help – the Holy Spirit of truth (John 15:26; 16:13). The Holy Spirit will guide us in all things. In the light of all that has been given to us, let us be vessels fit for the Master's use (2 Timothy 2:21), marked by dedication to His service in the locality where He has placed us, so that the testimony be blessed and bright. Let us pray that, in our day, the Lord will also raise up those in the local assembly who uphold the truth which has been delivered, who are guided by the Holy Spirit, and who are dedicated to the Lord to maintain the testimony and to serve His people.

## GROUP 5 – THE TREASURERS (VERSES 24-36)

Verse 24 tells us that it was to Sherebiah, Hashabiah and ten of their brethren that the silver and gold were entrusted. It was all carefully weighed and recorded as it was passed over to these men who were separated to this task. Ezra reminds the group (verse 28) of the position of trust and of dignity that was now theirs, "You are holy", and the vessels entrusted to them were holy. Ezra emphasises the importance of their task with the words "Watch…keep" (verse 29).

Paul similarly reminded Timothy of the special task that was his in his day (2 Timothy 1:13,14). That same challenge is ours today! How do we measure up to the tasks with which we have been entrusted? How do we handle the Lord's treasures? 2 Timothy 2:2 reminds us of our obligation to ensure that what has been given to us is faithfully passed on to others for future generations. Today, we need to watch out for savage wolves (Acts 20:29), for ravenous wolves and, more especially, for those in sheep's clothing (Matthew 7:15). As those men of Ezra's day had to guard against robbers and bandits, so we need to guard against those who would rob us of what has been entrusted to us for our safekeeping and which rightly belongs to the Lord.

This group consisted of twelve men. It was representative of all Israel, not just the remnant gathered by the river of Ahava. This should encourage us today. God still has those in the church who will carry out the task of caring for His treasure. The names of the four men mentioned at the completion of the journey are instructive: Meremoth, 'strong, firm'; Eleazar, 'God helps'; Jozabad, 'Jehovah endows'; and Noadiah, 'Jehovah assembles'. These four meanings should characterise those amongst the people of God who have been entrusted to look after the treasure, not only that of God's word but also of the material and financial gifts of the assembly.

In Scripture, number four can speak of testing. These four men waited until the fourth day (verse 33) before handing over their charge. There was no desperate attempt to be rid of the great responsibility that they carried. Everything they did was measured. The initial charge given to them in Ahava was that the task was holy, they were holy, and the articles for which they were responsible were holy. So we need to realise that those who have responsibilities in the local gatherings are handling that which the Lord calls holy. Are we sometimes careless how we handle the financial, spiritual and welfare aspects of the local assembly?

For these four men, the daunting task, as well as the awesome responsibility, of safeguarding the treasure was now over. There was nothing lost! The weights were identical! What a relief it must have been as they handed over the silver and the gold and the vessels! All these were necessary for the furtherance of the worship of the Lord in Jerusalem. Today, also, we have many responsibilities as we look after that with which we have been entrusted – the upkeep of the fabric of the place in which we meet; the legal aspects of trusteeship; the distribution of financial help.

Now that their responsibility was discharged, it was time to rejoice. In verse 35, we see that the people flocked to the altar to offer their thanksgiving with a great number of burnt offerings. The burnt offering speaks of all that was for God; neither the priest nor the offerer had any part of it. How wonderful when we realise that all our blessings come from God and then to respond by giving Him the praise and worship of which He is so worthy!

Twelve he-goats were offered as a sin offering. The returning people identified with their brethren, all Israel, as a people who had failed in their responsibility to God. We, too, should realise this as we look at Christendom today and humble ourselves because of the failure all around – not just in Christendom generally but in ourselves.

The treasurers then fulfilled their responsibility to those who were not of Israel: the king's satraps and governors – the powers that be. So we are reminded that we should pray for all in authority that we should lead "a quiet and peaceable life in all godliness and reverence" (1 Timothy 2:2, NKJV).

What a scene it must have been! Joy, contrition, thankfulness and worship all blended together there. The whole company, those 1,700 souls, were finally in the court of the temple, praising and thanking God for His goodness and mercy shown to them. They were now able to sing the Lord's song in His courts. They were no longer those who wept as they longed for this moment when in the strange land (Psalm 137), but were now in a place of nearness. It may be that the vast crowd took up the Songs of degrees (Psalms 120-134) as they made their way to the temple. We, too, should take up our songs of praise for the Lord's great blessings to us as we come into His presence – not only for the blessings experienced along life's way, but those of forgiveness, redemption, justification, reconciliation. We will grow to appreciate these more as we look into the scriptures, those treasures which have been faithfully preserved and handed down to us in our day.

# Chapter 9:
# Ezra's resource

There are many similarities between Nehemiah chapter 9, Daniel chapter 9 and this chapter but comparisons are not the subject before us here. The important features of this chapter are the disappointment, the resolve and the resources of Ezra. Here is a man who "through the good hand of God", with his companions, had just safely completed an extremely arduous journey. Faithfulness and dependency on the Lord were their hallmark. At the end of chapter 8, they had offered to God their burnt offering in thanksgiving for His goodness. They would be on 'a spiritual high'.

What a disappointment it must have been, then, for Ezra when he was suddenly confronted with the state of things in Jerusalem, God's centre! Well might he be astonished (verse 3)! He had come to Jerusalem expecting to find things different from those he had left behind in Persia. He expected to find a people who were obedient to the word of God and who were faithful in His service, who had separated themselves from the defilement that was around them, and who were thankful for the way God had preserved them through the captivity.

Today the church is faced with similar problems which are largely man-made, basically reflecting a lack of obedience to God's word. Our thoughts, and what we think to be most expedient, often prevails in assembly life, home life, and work life – those three important spheres of life that the Apostle Paul addresses in his letter to the Colossians. Do we, as we look around today, experience sadness when we see believers happily doing what is contrary to God's word, or do we go on as if there is nothing to be concerned about?

"The position of gathering to the name of the Lord in simplicity as members of the one Body is not one in which there is no trouble. Far from it! But it is the place where all trouble can be set right and every difficulty met by the word of God alone; this cannot be said of any sect in Christendom" (H. A. Ironside). Ezra was concerned about the situation facing him. Chapter 9 shows us many attributes of his that we could well emulate.

## THE LISTENING MAN

In verses 1,2 we see Ezra as the listening man. The princes inform him of the amalgamations of the people, the Levites, and the priests with the nations around. Ezra did not say to the princes, "I have no time. This is your problem; deal with it yourselves." Today, we live at a pace unique in this world's history. Because of this and the consequent emphasis on materialism (time is money), there is a need for believers to make time to listen to the problems of others. This could also be used to bridge the distance between believers and unbelievers in this needy world.

This ability to listen does not give license to be a busybody (1 Timothy 5:13). Ezra did not go around looking for problems. That grave problem was brought to him. Israel had been instructed concerning their relationships with the nations surrounding them (see Exodus 34:10-16). The church today also has instructions as to relationships with this world. We should not be unequally yoked together with unbelievers (2 Corinthians 6:14). This applies socially as well as intimately. Believers have been led astray by having leisure and professional links with unbelievers.

## THE AFFECTED MAN

As Ezra listened, he was very much affected by what he heard. He could easily have said, "This is no concern of mine. I've just arrived in Jerusalem", and left the problem to the locals to deal with and put right. But no! In verse 3, we find Ezra deeply distressed. He sat down astonished! The root cause of the conditions prevailing in Jerusalem went right back to the time of Esau, who took wives from among the Canaanites (Genesis chapters 27,28). Numbers chapter 25 is a vivid reminder of this recurring problem. Prior to the captivity, it had become such a chronic problem that the only remedy was drastic judgment from God. The people of Israel had endured 70 years in exile as a result of the idolatry which the mixed marriages had brought upon them. Sadly, that same problem appears here again.

Some of the leaders had turned a blind eye to the evil; others had either participated in it or condoned it. But some were deeply concerned by it. We may not have to contend with this particular problem today, but there are others, equally serious, which face us. How are we affected by them? Are we like some of those who participated, condoned or turned a blind eye? Or are we also deeply concerned by them? Ezra was so much affected that he tore his clothes and plucked out some of his hair. Others could see his concern. He was affected physically by the sad state of affairs prevalent in Jerusalem – he had to sit down (verse 3). We, too, need to be equally concerned at what is going on in the church today.

## THE CONSPICUOUS MAN

In verse 4, we read that the contrite of the people assembled unto Ezra. They came to God's man of the moment. He would be very conspicuous there, sitting in the street with his torn garments in obvious distress. This was the man whom God had just used to bring another group of Jews safely from Babylon with a vast amount of treasure for the temple. What a sight he must have been! This vista of God's servant, Ezra, reminds us of another Man who was conspicuous. Pilate said to the crowd, "Behold the man!" (John 19:5). But the crowd cried, "Away with Him". There gathered around Ezra those who "trembled at the words of the God of Israel" (verse 5). We can thank God that even today there are those who reverently fear the Lord and who gather together unto Him.

The people in Ezra's day realised the seriousness of the situation around them and identified themselves with Ezra. Are we aware of the situation around us and what are we doing about it? Ezra sat astonished until the evening sacrifice, having fasted all day. God still says, "To this man will I look, even to him that is poor (or, humble) and of a contrite spirit, and trembleth at my word" (Isaiah 66:2). Do these qualities characterise us, or are we, like some in the profession of Christianity, unaffected by that which is abhorrent to God and who actually condone and promote wanton sin because it is prevalent in today's society? God forbid that it be so!

## THE OVERCOMING MAN

Ezra got up at the time of the evening sacrifice (verse 5). That evening sacrifice, the burnt offering, reminds us of the death of our Lord. It was that which fully delighted and satisfied the heart of God. In Ezra's day, it looked on to the Lord's death. Ezra knew that this was the time and place where relationships with God were both made and restored.

Ezra knew that he alone could do little about the situation. He realised the value of communion with God. He remembered his journey from Ahava and the way God's hand had been over them in that perilous journey. He falls to his knees and spreads out his hands before the Lord (verse 5). Ezra knew where his resources lay. They were in God! "Who is he who overcomes the world, but he who believes that Jesus is the Son of God?" (1 John 5:5, NKJV). Ezra brings his problem to the Lord and tells Him about it. We have that same resource and are encouraged to bring our problems to the Lord instead of trying by ourselves to sort them out.

## THE CONFESSING MAN

Verses 6,7 depict Ezra's deep sorrow and his confession of sin to God, though himself personally blameless. The failure of the people to separate themselves to God could not be laid at Ezra's door. He had only just arrived and been told of the behaviour of the people of the land. He does not stand aghast at the wrong as though it was nothing to do with himself, but identifies with that wrong and makes it his confession.

He was too ashamed to lift up his face towards the Lord. In his prayer, he tells the Lord how he saw the situation. He says, "Our iniquities have risen higher than our heads, and our guilt has grown up to the heavens." What a situation! There seemed to be no way out. That was not all. Ezra goes further back into history and confesses that this sin went right back to "the days of our fathers".

We, too, live in a day of failure but often behave as though we are unaffected by it. Church history teaches us that there was failure from the beginning. The Lord had to charge the church at Ephesus with leaving their first love (Revelation 2:1-7). We do not find in Scripture or secular history that full recovery ever took place. Today, in this day of breakdown, we need to emulate Ezra, being concerned and ashamed of the current conditions, identifying with them and confessing them before the Lord.

## THE APPRECIATIVE MAN

In the next two verses, Ezra appreciates the grace of God: "And now for a little while grace has been shown from the LORD our God" (verse 8). Here we are reminded how God had showed His unmerited love and kindness to a wayward people. Ezra recalls that they were but a remnant – "a peg in His holy place". Isaiah 22:23 (NKJV) reminds us of "a peg in a secure place", that which could be relied upon – Christ Himself. Isaiah's prophecy looks on to the time when the Lord will be glorified here on earth in the nation He had chosen. In the grace of God, a partial fulfilment had taken place in the days of Ezra and Nehemiah. God's people had returned to Jerusalem; the temple had been rebuilt; worship was once more taking place.

Today, in this day of breakdown, we can also have a similar assurance that a nail has been put in a secure place. Truths, such as the personal return of the Lord for His church, once lost have been re-established; privileges once denied have been restored. We can enjoy the simplicity of gathering unto the Lord's name and functioning as kings and priests unto God.

Ezra appreciated what God had done for His people. He refers to God's mercy in freeing them from slavery, and being once more established in Judea and Jerusalem (verse 9). We, too, need to appreciate all that the Lord has done for us. We have, in Christ, far more than Israel had in Ezra's day but we may not always appreciate our blessings and privileges. The Apostle Paul, writing to the Ephesian Church, cannot restrain himself from bursting into praise as he informs the church what blessings they have in Christ (Ephesians 1:3-14). These blessings are still the same because they are in Christ, the one who is unchangeable, and what is more, they are ours today. Let us realise the wonder and the greatness of the truth that has been passed down to us. When we do, blessing will follow.

## THE REMEMBERING MAN

In veses 10-12, Ezra remembers the commandments of the Lord and admits that Israel has forsaken them. During his day of sitting astonished, Ezra would have had ample time to go over the instructions given by God to Moses. God had stated that the land was polluted by idolatry, full of abominations and totally unclean. Strict instructions had been given to the Israelites about relationships and the need to keep the inheritance pure.

Do we remember what we were taught regarding the things of the world and being unequally yoked to it? Are we contaminated by the spirit of the age and prepared to let things slide? Like Ezra, we need to look around and see the confusion that surrounds us. Then let us ask the Lord to show us what part we can play in it. The testimony is almost broken down and in a very weak state. But recovery is possible! Our part is to be wholly separated unto the Lord, to be faithful to His word, and to serve Him here in maintaining the testimony and promoting the glorious Gospel of God. Ezra remembered the old paths and sought to walk in them. We should follow his example.

## THE RESPONSIBLE MAN

We see this characteristic in verses 13,14. Ezra acknowledges the failure and identifies himself with it. What a lesson for us today! We are often ready to see faults and failures in other groups of Christians, behaving like the Pharisees did, when we should be contrite before God. Each Christian is part of the Christian testimony in the world. Ezra, in spite of having just arrived in Jerusalem, accepted the blame and the guilt of his fellow Israelites. We, too, need to accept responsibility for our part in the breakdown we see around us and the shame which that has brought to the testimony of the church. We have in Christ great privileges, but we also have equivalent responsibilities. Failure to realise our responsibilities will cause further harm to the testimony.

Ezra recognises in his prayer that God had dealt graciously with His people, despite their great failure. In this day of breakdown, we too can still see God's hand of grace bestowing blessing upon a church that, from its earliest days, has brought shame to her blessed Lord. In Revelation 3:14-22, we see the Lord's judgment on the church's failure, but we also see His wondrous grace: "If anyone hears My voice and opens the door, I will come in to him and dine with him, and he with Me." In verse 2, we are instructed "to strengthen the things which remain" and in 2:25 to hold fast what we have until the Lord comes.

Let us take up the challenge and the responsibility of these exhortations. When we come together, it will then be with ready and prepared hearts so that our worship of the Lord will flow freely and not be constrained by undue coldness and silence. Let's show something of Ezra's character in our day. If we do not, the Lord has a right to take away our lampstand (Revelation 2:5, NKJV).

## THE CONTRITE MAN

In the last verse of the chapter, we read of Ezra's deep contrition. We get a real sense of the shame and sorrow that he was enduring: "O LORD God of Israel, You are righteous, for we are left as a remnant, as it is this day. Here we are before You, in our guilt, though no one can stand before You because of this". All that is left for Ezra and that remnant is the mercy of that righteous God. Let us ever remember these attributes of the Lord our God!

On Mars Hill, Paul reminds the Athenians that in God "we live and move and have our being" (Acts 17:28). God is central to our being. Though we know Him as our Father, let us always remember His supremacy, that He is righteous, that He is Just, and that He abhors sin. We must never become familiar in our dealings with Him. Our relationship with Him started at Calvary's cross, that place where, as individuals, we were contrite for our sins. That was where we found forgiveness, rest and peace. In His grace, He has given a place of nearness and security. We need to express our gratitude with thanksgiving and praise.

Let us, like Ezra, accept the responsibility of the failure around us and cast ourselves on the Lord's mercy and grace.

# Chapter 10:
# Ezra – the man of action

In this last chapter of the book of Ezra, we see the reaction of the people, the sorrow and fortitude of Ezra, and the response of a leader of the people in a day when all seemed lost. What a picture is before us here! Sorrow and anguish seem to run throughout the chapter but, thanks be to God, it ends with restoration!

We, today, can take heart that, in spite of the abject failure of the remnant here, God provides the means of restoration. He has a "Man after His own heart"! If we are conscious of the sorrow we have caused Him, repenting of sin that so easily besets us (Hebrews 12:1), and are open to His instructions, we, too, can look forward to restoration. In this last chapter, as we focus on Ezra, his reactions and, in particular, his actions, we shall find many more lessons to consider.

## THE WEEPING MAN

In our day, we very rarely see a weeping man. Such a man, emotionally affected by what he sees, hears or comes in contact with, has a tender heart. In verse 1, we have such a man. Ezra was not ashamed to display his emotion publicly before the house of God. We should ask ourselves why we are not moved to tears when we look at the failure and breakdown that surrounds us. Sad to say, we are largely unmoved and take the attitude that we just have to get on with what is left. Here the people assembled to Ezra, weeping bitterly and repenting of their sin. It is very rare to see corporate repentance but seeing Ezra bowed down weeping had that effect on the people. Behind the scenes, as Ezra was weeping and praying, the Spirit of God was working in the hearts and consciences of the people to bring about restoration. We can thank God that His desire has always been to have a people after His own heart. Here we see the beginning of this in Ezra's day.

## THE SPOKESMAN

In verses 2,3, we see how Shechaniah speaks for the people when he identifies himself with the people's sin. Using words which must have brought some joy to Ezra, he says, "We have trespassed against our God, and have taken pagan wives". Shechaniah does not attempt to justify his or the people's actions. He realises that what was common practice amongst them violated the Law of God given by Moses. Today, in society in general, we also see that which was ordained of God being disregarded and, in many cases, set aside as being no longer expedient. Sad to say, we also see these trends in the assembly.

However, at the end of verse 2, we are reminded of hope but, before this hope was realised, there was to be a lot of grief and sadness. There are some things in life that cannot be put right by our actions, no matter how much we try. The grief and heartache that would be experienced by the heathen wives could not be alleviated in this life. It behoves us to be very careful in our dealings with unbelievers.

Shechaniah's confident hope was based on God's mercy. We today can express our hope with that same assurance. Hebrews 6:19 reminds us that we have such a hope as an anchor for our souls. Any hope of future blessing for these people was based on the fact that evil had to be manifested and judged in the putting away of the heathen wives. The principle still applies today. When judgment is made, action must immediately follow. Only then will God's mercy and grace flow out. Shechaniah now invites the people to make a covenant with God and to acknowledge the leadership of Ezra. We can thank God for the many today who preach the Gospel, inviting men and women to repent of their sins and acknowledge Jesus as their Lord.

### THE DEPENDABLE MAN

Shechaniah (whose name means 'the Lord is my neighbour') acknowledges on behalf of the people that they had found a man who was able to carry their burden (verse 4). Ezra was dependable – honest, trustworthy and upright. What a picture Ezra is of our Lord! Moreover, the people express their absolute confidence that Ezra was able to fulfil the awesome task before them: "This matter is your responsibility" (verse 4). They reinforce their affirmation by stating, "We also will be with you. Be of good courage, and do it" (verse 4). These words must have cheered Ezra's heart. The people identified themselves with him.

Today, we are asked to identify ourselves with our dependable Man. We are asked to show forth the Lord's death, till He comes. Are we regularly at the Lord's table? Do we each take up our privilege of telling Him that we are with Him? We will not do this by staying away at home, or week after week not opening our mouths in thanksgiving. That dependable Man, the Man of God's choosing, wants to hear from us. Years ago, as a young man and one of many in the assembly then, an older brother used to encourage us not only to attend but also to take part in the Breaking of Bread meeting. He brought to our attention part of that verse in the Song of Songs 2:14 "Let me see your face, Let me hear your voice" (NKJV); reminding us, that this also is the Lord's request to those He loves and that it was our privilege to respond to it.

That remnant had this one opportunity to affirm their allegiance to Ezra. We, too, have only this short time, "till He comes", to tell the Lord that we love Him and trust Him fully. Let us remember that it was for the joy that was set before Him that He endured the cross, despising its shame (Hebrews 12:2). The leaders of the priests, the Levites, and all Israel swore an oath that they would carry out the task before them (verse 5). Are we true to the commitment we made to the Lord Jesus to follow Him and to remember Him?

## THE BURDENED MAN

We now see the heavy burden that Ezra accepted on behalf of the people. Ezra takes himself out of the public spotlight and, in secret, he fasts and mourns because of the guilt of those from the captivity (verse 6). This burdened man did not make a show of the load that was placed upon him. We sing, "O Christ, what burdens bowed Thy head! Our load was laid on Thee." If Ezra suffered anguish in his day, how much more did Christ suffer for us in order to put right our wrong! We should be prepared to assist and to stand with those who are burdened about the weak and broken down testimony that exists today.

## THE AUTHORITATIVE MAN

Verses 7,8 show Ezra in a different light. Conditions were stated for restoration. What conditions they were! The people had three days in which to make their decision. It was either to join with Ezra and the leaders or suffer the extremely harsh consequences – their houses would be confiscated and they would be excommunicated. In other words, they would no longer be part of God's people.

Today, God's Man of authority speaks to this world, "I am the way, the Truth, and the Life" (John 14:6). There is no way to the blessing of knowing God as Father other than Christ's prescribed way. Note the reaction of the people! "All the people sat in the open square of the house of God, trembling because of this matter and because of heavy rain" (verse 9). The people realised the severity of the judgment and were deeply affected by it. We need to take heed to the words, "It is appointed for men to die once, but after this the judgment" (Hebrews 9:27, NKJV), and to allow them to have their full effect in our lives and upon our testimony.

## THE FEARLESS MAN

Ezra now stands before the people, reminding them of their sin and guilt before God and calling on them to make confession to the Lord God of their fathers (verses 10,11). Today, we can echo those words of Paul, "If you confess with your mouth the Lord Jesus and believe in your heart that God has raised Him from the dead, you will be saved" (Romans 10:9, NKJV). Preachers of the Gospel have to be fearless in whatever day they live. In days gone by, many suffered physical hardship; today it is likely to be ridicule and indifference. We thank God for those who are fearless in the preaching of the Gospel for it is the power of God unto salvation (Romans 1:16).

It also takes a fearless man or woman to follow the Lord and live for Him in today's society. Let us realise that He who is for us is greater than he who is against us (1 John 4:4). So let us go on to victory, showing our allegiance to our Lord and devotion to His will. We can take to heart the Lord's words to Joshua prior to the crossing of the river Jordan, "Be strong and of good courage; do not be afraid, nor be dismayed, for the LORD your God is with you wherever you go" (Joshua 1:9, NKJV).

## THE UNDERSTANDING MAN

Conditions were harsh. It was the rainy season, but the people affirmed "with a loud voice" (verse 12) that they would carry out what had to be done to put things right. However, because of the weather and the magnitude of the task that lay ahead, the people asked for more time (verses 13,14). Then we see the understanding man coming forth. Ezra did not reject their request out of hand nor was the task put off till a more convenient season. We see here a picture of the One who understands our weaknesses and infirmities – the One whose ear is ever open to our cry. The hymn writer puts it this way:

> *No one understands like Jesus.*
> *He's a friend beyond compare;*
> *Meet Him at the throne of mercy;*
> *He is waiting for you there.*

with the refrain:

> *No one understands like Jesus*
> *When the days are dark and grim;*
> *No one is so near, so dear as Jesus—*
> *Cast you ev'ry care on Him.*

Just as the remnant relied on Ezra, we can rely on our understanding Saviour!

## THE ORDERLY MAN

The task that had to be undertaken, as already stated, was massive. All the pagan wives had to be put away. The sin was in every corner of society – priests, leaders, and the common people. Romans 3:23 reminds us that all have sinned and come short of the glory of God. It would have been easy to group all the people together but, in verses 16,17, we find that careful investigation was made into individual circumstances. The investigations begin on the first day of the tenth month and last until the first day of the first month. Three months work! Mistakes could not afford to be made. It would have been tragic if a wife, of the seed of Israel, was unjustly put out of her house, home and family. This surely reminds us that we, in our day, have to be orderly in our dealings in assembly matters. It was not all left to Ezra – he had helpers in this onerous task (verse 16). What a shock it must have been to them when Jonathan opposed the ways of God and was backed up Meshullam and Shabbethai (see verse 15, NIV, JND trans.)! Meshullam had been one of Ezra's trusted companions (8:16). He was a man of credibility who was held in high esteem, but here we find him opposing God's will. Only when crisis occurs do we find out the true standing of others. The lesson for us in these verses is to be like the orderly man, not to jump to conclusions, and to expect shocks.

## THE RESTORING MAN

The chapter ends with a list of those who had taken heathen wives. Some of these had had children by them. We should remind ourselves that God records even our tears and keeps them in a bottle (Psalm 56:8). In this ignominious list of names, there were those who held places of privilege in the society of that day. They fell from grace.

However, even in this sad situation, the restoring man has the remedy. The priests are highlighted as those who gave their promise that they would put away their strange wives. An offering was made and restoration took place (verse 19).

Today, we have an Advocate with the Father (1 John 2:1) who can, and does, restore us when we fall. But we must first confess our sins (1 John 1:9). When we confess our sins, He is faithful and just to forgive us our sins and to cleanse us from all unrighteousness.

# Conclusion

The long list of names closes the record of Ezra and his God-given task to restore the remnant of Israel to be the people, chosen of God, to represent Him on earth. We can thank God that only a small proportion of the remnant is named as having gone astray. Even so, so far as the Lord is concerned, this was a serious matter.

We can see the same seeds of disaffection today. It can be termed the "my way" syndrome. We may not be looking for "strange wives" today, but we do like to have our own way. This wish, sadly, is not limited to home and work spheres; it is prevalent within the Christian fellowship and we suffer the consequences of it.

In Ezra's day, fellowship was restored. Today, we find that, because of the "my way" syndrome, there is little or no desire for restoration. Efforts that are made are continually being thwarted. We need to remind ourselves of our place, our privileges and our responsibilities as being amongst those who also are chosen and called by God (see Ephesians 1; 2 Peter 1). This act of grace was not for our blessing only, but that we should shine as lights in this world's darkness.

Throughout this book on Ezra, many lessons have been highlighted regarding our privileges and our responsibilities as those who seek to uphold a testimony for our Lord. As we have seen how God's mighty hand guarded and guided the people of God in Ezra's day, so let us rejoice that God's hand is still there to help us today. Let us take courage from that wonderful doxology of Jude: "Now to Him who is able to keep you from stumbling, and to present you faultless before the presence of His glory with exceeding joy, to God our Saviour, who alone is wise, be glory and majesty, dominion and power, both now and forever. Amen." (verses 24,25, NKJV)!

*LESSONS FROM EZRA*